Christian Challenges and Jokes

Robert Hillary

American Literary Press, Inc.
Five Star Special Edition
Baltimore, Maryland

Christian Challenges and Jokes

Library of Congress
Cataloging in Publication Data
ISBN 1-56167-457-5

Library of Congress Card Catalog Number:
97-078457

Published by

American Literary Press, Inc.
Five Star Special Edition
8019 Belair Road, Suite 10
Baltimore, Maryland 21236

Manufactured in the United States of America

Introduction

◼

My wife, Christell Hillary, and I believe that this book was inspired by the Holy Spirit to help encourage, and then put some laughs into, the lives of Christians as they take their daily walks with the Lord Jesus Christ. The stories presented in this book are ninety-five percent true and have been recalled to the best of our knowledge. Some of these stories will make you laugh, cry, think, and be encouraged. We dedicate this book to the Lord Jesus Christ, our Saviour and Redeemer. This work is also dedicated to the Drake and Hillary families.

Finders Keepers

———————■———————

Suppose you bought a house, and met the former owner just before moving in. The lady is in her nineties and she is being forced to sell her home and live with her son and daughter because of her age and mental capacity. She leaves a few things behind in the house when moving. The things she left behind are a few knickknacks, a bed and mattress, an old refrigerator and trunk with nothing of value in it . . . A week goes by and you decide to do some house cleaning. While moving the bed and mattress you notice that the mattress feels lumpy, you open the mattress and discover that it is stuffed with money. The bills are ten, twenty, fifty, and one hundred dollar bills. It all adds up to 150,000 dollars. You know it belongs to the old lady that owned the house before you. Now later on that evening you hear on the news that the old lady died of a heart attack. What do you do? The family is well to do, and there is no way anyone can trace the money. Do you give the money to her surviving relatives, her son and daughter? Or do you keep the money and say the Lord has blessed you? What?

The Decision

It's the Christmas season and you are coming from Bloomingdales where you have been doing some shopping. You're tired so you decide to flag or hail a taxi. You know it is going to cost you at least twenty or thirty dollars to get home, but you tell yourself you're tired and you have the money, so what the hey, you might as well. After about twenty minutes you get a cab. You get in the back seat and sit down to relax on your trip home. After riding for a couple of minutes you notice a small box on the floor of the cab. You pick it up and it's a jewelry box from one of the most exclusive diamond shops downtown. You open the box and discover a diamond ring inside worth at least 50,000 dollars. What do you do? Do you tell the cab driver that you found it and turn it over to him? Do you just put it in your pocket and say nothing? Do you turn it in at the nearest police station, knowing that after ninety days, if no one claims it, it's yours? Do you try to find the owner on your own? Or do you say to yourself, "God blesses in mysterious ways," and keep the ring for yourself? What?

The Fountain

 ―――――■―――――

You're a single woman or man in your sixties; you have the outward appearance of a person in his or her seventies. One day you go to the doctor and he examines you and comes back with bad news. He tells you that you have terminal cancer. You don't believe him so you get a second opinion from another doctor. He comes back with the same diagnosis. That you have "The Big C" and you have about a year to live. So you tell yourself that you are going to enjoy life the way the Lord wants you to. You quit your job, take some money out of the bank, and go on a vacation. You're a backpacker by hobby, so you rent a camper and some equipment for your vacation. After driving for a couple of days, through a couple of states you come across an isolated, mysterious lake. You get out and decide to take a swim. When swimming you instantly feel energized, like you could swim all day. Also while swimming you swallow some of the water. After about an hour, you get out of the water and start back on your way. You get back to the camper and start to dry off. You pass a mirror in the camper; you're startled and astonished at how you look. All your crows feet, lines, and wrinkles are gone. You also have regained the youthful appearance of a person in his or her forties. You decide you have discovered the legendary Fountain of Youth. You bottle some of the water and drive to the nearest doctor to find out what other changes have taken place. You find a good doctor. He examines you and comes back with a clean bill of health. The doctor says you're the finest specimen he has ever met in his life, and you don't have any cancer. Immediately you begin praising the Lord. Also you have a friend dying from AIDS, which he contracted through a blood transfusion he had years ago. You drive back home, he sees you, and asks you what happen to you. You tell him everything, leaving out where the lake is located. He tries some of the water and immediately he get better, no more AIDS. Now what do you do? Tell him where the lake located? Buy the land and make a profit off of it? Or just tell everyone where the lake is so they can receive the same blessing you have? What?

The Horse

———■———

Suppose you're a former backslider and your former lifestyle was that of a gambler. You just renewed your vows to the Lord and you feel good about yourself. Well, one day you're out on the street taking a walk to get some fresh air. While walking you run into an old friend, a person you use to gamble with in the old days. You greet each other and say hello, then the conversation comes around to horse racing. Your friend has a hot tip in the fifth race at Arlington Race Track. The horse's name is Precious Saint at fifty to one odds. Your old friend hands you two hundred dollars and a racing form. He says he can't go to bet on the horse because he's on his way to the hospital to visit his mother. He states the money from the horse will pay her hospital bills. He also further states that he will give you half the money for placing the bet for him and runs off before you can say anything else. Out of curiosity you look at the racing form to see who the horse is running against, and you come to the conclusion the horse has a 99.9% chance of winning. You think to yourself, if Precious Saint wins with the two hundred dollar bet, the winnings will be 10,000 dollars and 5,000 would be yours. Well, you have to go to work that day and your job is two blocks from the track. You could place the bet on the horse on your lunch break with no problem. Now gambling was a real habit for you in the past, what do you do? Place the bet for your old friend because he really needs the money? Pray about the matter. Decide not to place the bet because it could lead you back into your sin of gambling? Hold the two hundred dollars for him and say you couldn't do it because you're a Christian now? Or say to yourself, "This is a blessing and God works in mysterious ways," then bet. What is your decision?

The Ark

◼

It's the year 2,000. You buy a beautiful seven bedroom home. Also, you have been living there for about a year. Summer rolls around and you decide you want to do some gardening. You have a week's vacation. You also want to reseed the lawn and plant some roses. You know it's an all day job, so you get up early in the morning to start your task. While shoveling in your back yard, you dig deep and hit something hard and solid. You continue digging until you finally get it out of the ground. You examine it, and it is a small ancient chest from biblical days. You open it and find some parchment papers and scrolls inside. It looks like the papers are written in ancient Hebrew and also Greek. You have a friend that works downtown who knows about historic and ancient artifacts. So you decide to let him have a look at it. He takes a look at it, but doesn't know offhand exactly what it is. He takes pictures of the chest and the scrolls inside, then says he'll get back with you in a couple of days. You take the chest home and put it in the attic. Two days go by and you don't hear anything from your friend. On the third day the telephone rings. It's your friend who examined the chest. He is very excited. He tells you to sit down. You sit down and he tells you that the chest you found is the Ark of the Covenant, and that the papers inside are the genuine Old and New Testaments. He further states that he contacted some people that he knows and they have started bidding on your chest. The highest bid so far is one hundred million dollars. A museum also contacts you and wants you to donate the chest so everyone can see it. What do you do? Donate the chest and get nothing? Do you sell it for the one hundred million dollars? Do you just keep it for yourself? What?

The Ticket

———————————■———————————

Picture this in your mind. It's a bright sunny day, you're watching a good program on TV, relaxing, and enjoying the day. All of the sudden you hear a knock on the door. It's your neighbor Martha from downstairs. Well, you're a Christian. You have known her for ten years and she's not a Christian, but she's still a friend of yours. She comes to the door and asks how you are doing. You say you are blessed and you ask her to come in. You talk about the weather, your jobs, and other general things. Then Martha stops for a second and asks if you would do her a favor.

You think for a minute and say, "Sure I would. What is it?" She scrambles in her purse for a while and comes out with a long white sealed envelope. She asks if you would keep this envelope and apartment key for her until the next week. Well, you know Martha wouldn't do anything wrong and you agree to hold it until next week. Then Martha says that she and her husband Marty are going out of town on a vacation to California the following day and they would be driving. So you take the envelope from Martha and wish her a God filled vacation. You tell her to take plenty of pictures for you to see.

After Martha leaves you place the envelope on the dresser and think nothing else about it. Three days go by and the phone rings. It's Martha, she says that they're cutting their vacation short. She and Marty will be returning home soon. Another one or two days pass and you don't hear anything else from Martha. On the third evening the phone rings; it's a hospital calling from California about Martha and her husband Marty. The doctor asks, "Are you Mrs. _____, a friend of Martha?" You say, "Yes." He goes on to state that Martha and her husband died in a very bad traffic accident and that Martha put you down as her next of kin in case of an emergency. You're shocked and devastated. You try to get all the information from the doctor that you can. Then you start to call your job to get a couple of weeks off so you can make funeral arrangements.

You know that Martha and Marty don't have any living relatives; it's left up to you to do everything for your friend. So you take the key she left to her apartment. When you go in you immediately start to look for her insurance policy. After about and hour you find the policy and the policy is worth 15,000 dollars. It is also made out in your name and just enough to cover the arrangements for her and Marty.

Well, five days pass and you have taken care of all the funeral arrangements, the shipping of the bodies and everything. A couple more days go by and you remember the envelope Martha gave you to keep. You find it and open it. You look inside and it's a letter from your friend and five lottery tickets. Your friend says in her letter that if anything happens to her, and if the tickets win, keep the money for yourself. Just out of curiosity you check the tickets. The first four are losing tickets, but the fifth ticket is a winner. It's worth ten million dollars. You have never played the lottery in your life. Now, in your hand is a letter from your friend saying keep the money if it wins and a ten million dollar ticket. Tell me what would you do? Keep the money and pay tithes? Give it all to charity or just tear up the ticket? What would you do? Just think about it?

To Be Or Not To Be

■

Say that you're a very beautiful woman in your middle twenties, very light skinned, a mulatto black person. Anyone who sees you or talks to you would swear that you are white, but your mother is white and your father is black. Both are well educated and Christians. They have passed their lifestyle on to you. Well, you find a good secretarial job downtown in an all white office; no one knows that you're black. You take it for granted that your race doesn't matter, but you don't tell anyone.

After you have been on your job for about a year and have gotten to know people, you become particularly friendly with a lady named Jean and you start to eat lunch together and talk over the phone off and on for that whole year. You think you know her pretty well.

The last week in a month passes and you noticed that the company has hired someone else during your shift. The person is very black, the only other black person working for the company. You go over to talk to her and you find out that the new lady is a Christian. You talk about the Lord for a while and say you'll talk to her later because you have to get started working. Later, at lunch, you and Jean are eating and the new lady passes your table and says hello. Suddenly you notice Jean's reaction and the way she stares at the new co-worker. You smile at Jean and ask her what is wrong.

Jean looks you straight in the eyes, without blinking, and says, "I hate Negroes. Those black people are taking away all our jobs. But most of all I hate those Christians, someone needs to get rid of them all." You look at Jean in surprise and bewilderment. What do you do? Tell her that you're also black and a Christian? Don't say anything to Jean and never eat with her again? Give Jean a black eye right there at the table? Or quit your job? What do you think about it?

The Actress

———————————————— ■ ————————————————

Imagine that you're a handsome young man in your thirties and a good Christian. You have a good job, a house and a car. You are very successful and single, but you have been asking the Lord to send you a wife. This is the month of August, the last Sunday in the month, and you go to church like you normally do. You have met a lot of people in church over the years, men as well as women— some married but mostly single women. One woman in particular, by the name of Alice, is also single. You are sitting listening to the pastor preach one of his best sermons on deliverance, and the sermon lasts about an hour and a half. Keep in mind that it's a hot summer morning. It's about ninety seven degrees outside, and not too much cooler inside. Anyway, after the sermon is preached the pastor calls for all his altar workers to come to the front of the church. You go because you're on staff as one of the workers. It's you, another guy, and five other women. Then the pastor goes on to state, "If there's anyone who needs salvation or any type of deliverance, please come up." So you're standing there and you see Alice come up for prayer. She goes to one of the women altar workers, who prays out her soul for Alice's needs. They pray for about fifteen or twenty minutes, and they both finish up speaking in tongues. Alice gets ready to leave and walks past the five women and one guy, then gets to you. She shouts out she is going to faint, and faints right in your arms. What do you do or say? Call a doctor for Alice, or think maybe this is the wife that God has placed in your life? Tell Alice she needs to get back in line for further deliverance? Or don't say anything? What?

The Second Chance

OK, you're a little girl about ten years old. You have come to know the Lord at an early age, from your parents. You have a friend named Joan. She goes to school with you and you used to study and play with her every day. As you grow older, you and Joan move apart from one another, but you stay in light contact with each other over the years. Now, as the years go by you become a very beautiful woman in your mid-thirties, you have grown stronger in the Lord as the years have passed.

The Lord has blessed you in many ways through your life. You have a good career as a legal secretary, a house, a husband and two healthy boys. One day someone moves in the apartment building next door to you and, come to find out, it's Joan, your old childhood friend who you have not seen in fifteen years. You greet each other and Joan kisses you on the cheek and gives you a hug very strongly.

Well, she stays for about one year in the apartment next door, then she moves to another part of town. Before she moves, she gets your telephone number, gives you kisses on your cheek again, and says she'll keep in touch. During all this time Joan hasn't been saved or come to know the Lord as her personal saviour. Well, another two years pass and you haven't heard anything from Joan. Then early one Saturday morning the phone rings and it's her. She is in one of the neighborhood hospitals dying of AIDS from a homosexual lifestyle. She wants to see you because you have been a good friend over the years.

What do you do? Tell Joan to forget it you don't want to have anything to do with homosexuals, and you don't want to get AIDS? Send your minister to tell her about the Lord Jesus Christ? Or pray about it first and ask the Lord what you should do?

The Truth

You're a middle-aged woman, about fifty-one years old. As a Christian lawyer you have a successful law practice. For the last five years you have been defending people that have been victims of injustice. Well, one day a well to do man comes to your office and asks you to defend his teenage son, who he says is not guilty of the crime of murder. He knows his son did not commit murder. So you tell the man that first you would have to talk to his son and get the facts about the case before you say you'll take the case. Well, you go to the county jail to get information on the case and talk to the eighteen-year-old son, who is waiting for your arrival. Now, after getting the reports and speaking to the teenager you decide that the police have a very thin case against him. You talk to the father and tell him you'll take his son's case. You also talk to a friend of the boy that says he was with him twenty blocks away from the scene of the crime at the time the crime was committed. However, the courts have an eyewitness that says he saw the boy less than two blocks away from the scene at that time. Now, the boy doesn't have a criminal record of any kind so you believe and know that he's innocent. You get him out on bail and await the court date. Finally, a month later, the time to go to court arrives and everything is set. The prosecution states that the young man followed the elderly woman home and snatched her purse. During the process of robbery, the old lady slipped and fell, bumping her head on the concrete. She died. Now, you present your side of the case and show that the eye witness for the prosecution needs to wear glasses. He wasn't wearing them at the time of the crime, and he cannot be absolutely sure it was your client who committed the crime. The jury goes out for ten minutes, and you know your client will be acquitted of the crime. While the jury is out the boy whispers to you that he did kill the old lady. What do you do, being a Christian attorney? Tell the court he did commit the crime and that you don't want the case anymore? Or let him go scott free and say nothing? Or quit law altogether? You tell me what you would do?

The Gift

———————■———————

Suppose that you're a young man in your mid-twenties, and you're not a Christian, but you are married with two children. Let's say you have been married for about two years, with a job working at the steel mill for five years. One day in the middle of your two years of marriage, a co-worker who you have been partying with for some time asks you to try this drug he's been using called cocaine.

Well, at first you're reluctant to try it because you usually go out for a few beers and that's it. Your friend tells you how good it makes him feel, and how life seems a lot better when using cocaine. He ribs and teases you a while and calls you chicken. You tell him that your heart doesn't pump chicken soup and you try the drug. Well, after that you keep using the drug over a period of time. Your wife, who is a Christian, starts noticing a change in your habits. You're not the warm caring man she married years ago. Plus your style of dress has changed and you have started staying out all night. You start missing days at work.

Then the money from the savings and checking accounts is almost gone. One day, when you are coming in from work, your wife confronts you at the door with a small vile of white powder in her hand and asks you what it is. Reluctantly, you tell her it is cocaine and that you have been using it for a short time. You promise her that it's nothing you can't control and that you will stop using the drug. But you're hooked and can't stop. This goes on for another six months. Meanwhile, the company you work for makes it mandatory for everyone to take drug tests, but you can't stop using coke. A month later you take the drug test and fail. You lose your job.

You start searching for another job, but cannot find one right away. Meanwhile, your wife gets fed up and leaves with the two kids. She is going to stay with her mother until you can straighten out your life. However, the monkey is still on your back and you need money to pay for your habit. So you do things you thought you would never do in your life. You start selling everything you own and stealing. You even commit armed robbery. You also get involved in male prostitution—anything to get the money you need.

Well, eventually you end up in jail, busted for possession of cocaine. A family member bails you out and lets you stay with him. He's also a Christian. He talks to you about Jesus Christ, and you listen, but the devil brings that craving for coke back. So you take a walk along the beach to clear your head. While walking you begin to cry and picture your life the way it's been for the last few years. You cry and fall down on your knees, saying, "Lord Jesus, I am a sinner and I don't know you very well." You say, "Lord if you are real, please cleanse me and take this habit of cocaine, and help me to straighten out my life." Just then you hear a deep and audible voice saying, "Son, I have been with you always. I love you, and from this moment you aren't the same anymore."

You open your eye's to see if someone is playing a trick of some kind on you, but there's no one there. You get up and notice that the craving for coke is gone. You run back to your brother's house, who you have been staying with, and tell him the story. He tells you that you have heard from the Lord and that you are a new creature in Christ. Now, what do you do from here on? Join a church and start reading your Bible? Think someone was playing a trick on you? Or just say it was all in your mind? What, you decide?

Sink or Swim

———————■———————

Suppose that you're an active Christian woman in your early forties. You are married and you and your husband make a pretty good living for yourselves. You have been together for ten years. You don't have any children, but you and your husband love each other. You have not had a vacation together since you have been married. However, this year is different, you decided early in the year to take a vacation and you can get the same time off together. Well, one weekend you both sit down to plan your vacation. You decide that you would like to visit Hawaii for your two week vacation. Also, you decide to take a slow cruise to relax and forget your cares and worries.

You would also like to invite a Christian married couple you have known for years and with whom you have entered into a group life insurance policy. You talk to your friends and find out that they can get the same time off as you and your husband. They would be happy to join you on the cruise. Well the time rolls around and your vacation is all set—luggage, hotel, tickets, and spending money—everything. You and your husband pick up your Christian friends and set off for the ship. Once on board all four of you notice how beautiful the ship and your cabins are.

OK, the first night on board you and your husband have a heated argument about money and how some of your family members are always getting into your business. You always argue the same issues and neither one apologizes afterwards. That night your husband sleeps on the floor in the washroom. Well, the next night comes around and you both are still mad about what the other said the night before. You decided to hide it because you don't want your Christian friends to know you have been fighting. Well that night it is stormy, but all four of you decide to take a walk together on deck. While walking on deck a big wave of water knocks all four of you overboard with a raft, which only holds two people. Now between the four of you, you are the only one that can swim. Also, the group insurance policy that all of you have states that if anyone of you dies the surviving persons shall collect the money from the policy.

Now, getting back to the situation at hand. All of you are in the water, you make it to the raft. You're looking in the water, your husband and your Christian friends are going down for the third time. What do you do in a situation like this? Save your husband, with whom you are still angry? Save just one of your Christian friends? Let all of them drown and collect on the insurance policy? What have you decided?

Dad

———■———

Suppose you're a Christian man, saved, spirit-filled, speaking in tongues, and everything. Your family members are saved, also. You have a beautiful wife and kids, a nice career as an engineer, and life couldn't be more wonderful. The only problem is that your father is not saved and doesn't know the Lord Jesus Christ as his personal saviour. Your mother, however, is saved and knows the Lord. Every now and then you try to witness to your father about the Lord Jesus Christ. All he says is that one day he'll accept the Lord, but right now he's enjoying life too much.

Well, one winter day when you father is driving to his friend's house his car goes out of control and hits a tree. Your father is rushed to the local hospital and your mother calls to tell you the whole story and asks you to meet her at the hospital. When you get to the hospital your mom is there and the doctor tells you that your father is clinically dead. His heart has stopped functioning, but his brain is still working with the help of machines. He is also using a breathing machine. You and your mother go into a waiting room to pray. Both of you pray out of your hearts and souls to the Lord for your father, who is being kept alive by a life supporting machine.

Now, your father and mother are retired and they receive Medicare and small retirement checks. As the years pass, your father is still hooked up to the machines that are keeping him alive. The medical insurance that your father has doesn't cover all of the medical bills for him. Your mother doesn't have any more money, so you help with all your savings that you have. Remember, all this time you have not stopped praying for your father. One day after work your mother calls and asks to see you. You rush right over to see her. She explains to you that she loves your father very much and they have had many happy times together. Then she pauses for a minute and asks you to do something for her. You say, "Anything, Mom." She says that your father's memory is deep inside her, but she can't stand seeing your father hooked up to those machines any longer. She wants you to go to the hospital the following day and disconnect your father from the machines so he can go on to be with the Lord. She is not strong enough to do this herself. You don't answer, but leave with your head hanging down.

What do you do in a situation like this? Do as your mother requested? Seek the Lord even harder for your prayers? What have you decided to do? Also I have another question to ask. Do you believe in euthanasia?

Insensitivity

———————————————— ■ ————————————————

Well, you're a young woman in your early thirties. You're a Christian and you met the Lord when you were a teenager. You have been married for about seven years and you have two children, six and seven years old. Your husband has a good job as an airline pilot for one of the major airlines. Remember, you and your husband are saved and you try to impress your beliefs on the children so they can grow up knowing Jesus for themselves.

All right, one day you and your husband get into a big argument about your spending too much money. He calls you a silly woman that doesn't know how to handle money. You march off hotter than a firecracker in July to your prayer room to seek the Lord on this matter. You stay there for a couple of hours, just talking to the Lord, and come out a little cooler than you went in.

Now, it's about dinner time and you call the kids downstairs to eat. They come and so does your husband. You tell him that you are sorry about the way you handle money and that you will try to do better in the near future. He says, "OK, what's to eat." You prepare the kids' dinner and place it before them, but while you are fixing your husband's dinner something comes to mind. In all the years you have been married and after all the arguments you both have had, never once has he said to you that he was sorry for anything he has done or said. You start to get angry again. What do you do in this situation? Take his dinner you have prepared for him and pour it over his head? Bring up the matter at the dinner table or wait until the kids go to bed and bring it up? Go back to your prayer room and pray for your husband who is very insensitive? Or don't say anything about it? What would you decide? Remember, there are two things hard for a man to say— one is "I love you" and the other is "I'm sorry."

The Beast

All right, you're a married man in your early twenties. You have a good job as a clerk carrier for the post office. You are also a good Christian and a family man. You have worked all year round and you have about three weeks vacation coming to you. So, you and your wife get together to decide where you would like to spend your vacation. Your wife wants to spend the time in sunny Florida. It's the middle of winter in the city where you are, and she wants to go somewhere warm and beautiful. However, your desire is to go backpacking and camping in the mountains. This would bring back some of the good old times you use to have as a young man camping again. So, you compromise with your wife and say that if she spends five days with you out in the wilderness, you'll spend the rest of the time in Florida with her. Your wife looks at you like you are a little crazy, but agrees to the arrangement.

Now, vacation time comes around and everything is ready—the camper, sleeping bags, backpacks, maps, all of which you have rented for your vacation. You decide to go camping in Arizona. After driving for a day and a half, you make it to your destination. Your wife looks around and notices how beautiful the scenery is and how peaceful and quite it is out in the wilderness. That night you and your wife make wonderful love together like never before and your wife falls asleep. But for some reason you just can't go to sleep. You think maybe it is just the excitement of camping again. You lay down and

27

think of how beautiful the day has been.

Around 1:00 a.m. you hear something or someone rustling through the trees not far from the camper. You get up, grab the flash light and your 38 caliber revolver from the glove compartment and leave your wife sleeping. You walk over to where you believe the noise came from and shine your flashlight. You look for a minute and see nothing. Suddenly, just as you turn to go back to the camper you see something big and hairy in the bushes. It stands up—about eight feet tall—and looks you straight in the eyes from about five feet away. You're so afraid that you forget you have the gun in your hands. The first word that comes out of your mouth is "Bigfoot." Just then snow starts to fall heavily. Bigfoot looks at you, and you at him for a minute, and then turns and runs off into the trees. You stand there for another minute or so because you just can't believe there really is a Bigfoot. Then you run back to the camper, where your wife is still sound asleep, and wake her up. You drag her outside, telling her the story as you go. By the time you get outside, all of the tracks are gone. Because of the falling snow there is no trace of Bigfoot.

Now, your wife stares at you and smells your breath to see if you have had something to drink stronger than Kool-Aid. She tells you to go back to the camper and go back to sleep. You must have been dreaming. What do you do? Try to make her understand you really did see Bigfoot? Stay that whole week searching for your Bigfoot to prove it to your wife? Say it was the devil trying to trick you and pray about it? Pick up everything and get the heaven's name out of that place? Or decide your wife was right, you were dreaming? What would you decide?

The Big Problem

■

OK, you're a married man, and you and your wife are saved Christians. You have three children and their ages are thirteen, sixteen, and twenty-two. You've had a semi-wonderful life up to this point. I mean your marriage has been all right for the five years you have been together. You love your wife and have known her since grade school eighteen years ago. You are a factory worker downtown, and your wife works at the church on staff at the nursery school.

Over the years you have come to know your wife and children very well. You love all of their different personalities. However there is only one problem. Your wife spends most of her time at the church. Whenever they need someone to volunteer for something your wife is always up front and ready. She spends so much time there that they should change the name of the church to her first name. She works so hard that she doesn't have enough time for your family's needs. One evening you confront your wife and tell her how you feel about her cleaning up the church and not cleaning the house. Also, you tell her of your need for her as a wife. "Please don't get me wrong," you say, "doing things at the church and for the Lord is beautiful, but you have to have balance in your life."

Your wife doesn't want to listen to you and the conversation leads to a big argument about things you never even thought about before. The argument carries on and gets around to the kids. She says only one of the kids is really yours and that you hate the thirteen-year-old and the six-year-old. (Two of the children came from a relationship that she was in before your marriage.)

You are deeply hurt by what she just said. You try not to show it, but it hurts bad. You have come to love all of your children and try not to see any difference between them. You walk away, not knowing what to say. What do you do from here? Pray for a while about the matter? Just tell your wife that she hurt you when she said that? Or just let it roll off your back because your wife is always saying things she doesn't really mean? What would you decide?

The Neighbor

---■---

Suppose you're a saved Christian man and have been married for about fifteen years. You have also been with the Lord for about the same length of time. You have two teenage kids, fourteen and fifteen years old, and you and your family have lived a good Christian life until now. You had a good job as a policeman up until last year when you retired. As a cop on the police force you handled domestic problems and violence as a Christian, the way the Lord would want. You thank the Lord that none of the situations you saw as a police officer ever affected your family.

Well, one day you are out visiting your policemen friends at the station. Suddenly you get the feeling you should return home. On returning home you find your wife on the couch crying heavily about something. You go to her and ask what is the matter or problem. She looks very deeply at you and says nothing, then she runs into the bathroom and closes the door. She returns, trying to hide her feelings, and goes to the kitchen to prepare dinner. But she drops the plates and glasses and breaks them on the floor. You run to the kitchen to find out what is really the problem with your wife. Again she says nothing, just a program on television worried her. Just then your two teenage sons return home from school, so you drop the subject for now. You all have dinner and retire to bed. As you and your wife lay down to sleep, your wife seems distant from you. She doesn't even want to make love to you. This goes on for about a week until you can't stand it anymore. You find yourself going out for a walk each day, and every day that you go out, you run into your neighbor Sam, who lives across the hall from your apartment. He asks how are you doing says tell your wife he said hello. He does this in a very strange way, but you don't think anything of it and go on about your business, worrying about the problems at home. OK, you've been out about two hours walking on the fifth day and you realize that you keep forgetting to tell your wife that good neighbor Sam said hello. When you get home, you tell your wife that Sam said hello but you kept forgetting to tell her. Just then your wife becomes hysterical and cries. You run to her and shake her and demand that she tell you what the problem is.

She breaks down and says, "Last week while you were gone to the station, our neighbor Sam came over and said his phone just went out and he had to make an emergency telephone call. I didn't see any harm in it, so I said, 'Sure come in.' When he got inside our apartment he pulled me down and raped me on the couch. I was so ashamed that I didn't tell you for fear of losing you and the life we've had together."

You turn your back and begin to cry yourself and all kinds of thoughts are running to your head. This man is the man that you have been seeing and who has been smiling at you. And he has raped your wife.

Now, tell me what you would do as a Christian? Remember, you're a man first and a Christian second— but God's man all the way. What do you do? Kill him? Call your policemen friends and have him arrested? Do you pistol whip him with a 38 caliber revolver or go rape his wife? Pray about it and tell me seriously what you would do.

The Singer

■

You are a Christian family man and you and your wife are saved. About a year or two into the marriage the Lord blesses you with a son. Both of you are so happy and praise the Lord for your blessing. You know that your son is going to make a difference in this world. At an early age, about five or six, you start giving him piano and singing lessons.

Your son grew up well and he's about twenty years six months old now. He has stayed with the lessons you gave him and has a good Christian background. Plus, the most important person you want him to know is Jesus Christ. Your son starts singing gospel music in the church band and choir. He sounds so good that the pastor gives him the spot of lead or head singer and musician. I mean your son is so good, that you glorify and praise the Lord each time you hear him sing or play and the pastor begins to make gospel records of your son. He also makes an excellent profit for the church.

OK, it's time for Sunday morning services and your son sings a solo especially for you and the Lord. Your son sings to say thank you for all you have done in his life. Until this time you and your son have had a very good relationship, with Jesus at the center. He plays his song, and about two hours later the service is over. The people begin to go up and congratulate your son on his performance, ability, and talents. You start to walk over to your son to talk to him, but before you get to him one of the members of the church stops you to say hello. You say hello to the member and smile, but your mind is on your son. You glance over and see him talking to a very well dressed stranger. They talk a while and the stranger gives your son a small white business card. The stranger pats him on the back and then leaves. Just then your conversation with the church member is over, so you say good-bye and walk over to your son. You hug your son, as a Christian father would do, and thank him for the song he sang. Then you ask who the stranger he was talking to was and what he wanted. Your son looks at you and says with a smile, "That was Mr. Burns, a rock music promoter from one of the major rock music companies here in the U.S. He wants me to sign a contract for the next five years to sing secular music and I'll be making thirty-two million dollars a year." You say, "Naturally you told him you were a Christian and said no to his offer." Then your son tells you that he told Mr. Burns that he would think about it and get back with him in a few days. But you know your son and the Christ within him so you don't worry. A week goes by and you talk to your son again. He says he is going to accept Mr. Burns' offer to sing secular music. Your son also states that the money is too good to pass up and he's tired of being a poor Christian. You try to talk him out of it, but his mind is made up. He'll be leaving for California in a few days. You walk away feeling sad for him and yourself. What do you do? Pray about it, then go back and talk to him until he sees the errors of his ways? Keep in mind that he's almost twenty-one years old and he can make his own decisions. What do you decide?

The Employee

■

OK, you are a Christian supervisor at one of the largest well known printing companies downtown. One day you come into work to discover that your boss has hired a new employee. Just by looking at him and talking to him you come up with the idea that he might be gay. Well, you don't pay any attention to your thoughts and you go on with your duties as a supervisor. A few days go by and you start to hear rumors about the new employee, stories that he wears women's clothes under his men's clothing and that the men in the locker room are teasing him and feeling his bottom. A few more days pass and the stories keep coming.

One day you run into the new employee coming into work and you get into a long conversation. He tells you that he is a homosexual and has been one since he was fifteen years old. He is very proud to be gay and says you should try him out sometime. Well, you're very surprised at his attitude and try to talk to him about Jesus. Then he smiles at you and says that whenever you get tired of that Jesus kick and women to come see him and he will help you to see what life is all about. Well you walk away, shaking your head and praying for the man.

You know that if he stays in the men's locker room there will be more trouble and stories. So what do you do about the situation? Go to your boss and tell him that the new employee is a homosexual and get him fired? Start letting him change clothes in the women's locker room?

Find a private office or place for him to change clothes? Or don't say anything about it and let the situation run its own course—your boss will find out for himself? Continue talking to the man about Jesus and praying for him? What do you do? The decision is up to you. But remember, you are still a Christian.

The Beggar

—■—

Put yourself in the place of this person. You're a married man who works at the post office as a mail handler and you're a good Christian family man. You also have three children—two boys and a girl. Their ages are five, six, and seven years old. You have been married for about eight years.

You meet one of your neighbors on the street and you strike up a conversation. You talk about Jesus and how nice the day is. Well, at the end of your talk with your neighbor he asks you for some change to get on the bus. You don't see any harm in it and you want to be a good Christian, so you give him sixty cents to get on the bus. The next day you run into the same guy and you get into another conversation. He tells you that he used to be on drugs but all that has changed since he's met Jesus. Again, he asks you for some change, this time to get coffee. Again you reach into your pocket, pull out some change, and hand it to him. He says good-bye and off to work you go, thinking nothing of it. After work you go home, have your dinner, play with the kids and wife, and go to bed. At about three o'clock in the morning the doorbell rings (you have to get up at 7:00 a.m.). You go to the door and it's your neighbor, the man you gave change to twice before. You open the door and ask him what he wants this early in the morning. He says he is sorry for waking you up so early in the morning, but it's an emergency. He says his mother has just gone into the hospital and he doesn't have any money to go see her. He wants to know if he could borrow five dollars until tomorrow. You, being a Christian, believe the story and run to get your wallet and hand him the money.

Well, the next day arrives and your neighbor hasn't come with the five dollars he owes you. Weeks pass and you haven't heard a word from him Then one day you run into him on the street, and you are about to ask about the five spot he owes you. Before you can say anything he tells you that he has just lost his job and has just gotten out of jail. He says he hasn't forgotten that he owes you five dollars. He then asks you for a couple of dollars because he is hungry and doesn't have anything to eat. He will pay you, he says, as soon as he gets back on his feet again. Once again you have the milk of human kindness and give him a few dollars.

This happens off an on for about a year—the early morning visits, the emergencies, the sob stories. Each time it's a different story and each time you are out of a few dollars. One day you meet him on the street and talk to him. He tells you he still hasn't found a job yet, so you tell him the post office has a position open for a janitor and that you could put in a good word for him with your supervisor. He could be working in just a couple of days you tell him. However, as soon as you get this out of your mouth, the man says he doesn't do that kind of work and he likes working odd jobs outside where he feels free. He says thanks to you and walks off in a hurry.

Then the next time he sees you he has another sob story to tell you and he borrows a few more dollars until the end of the week when he gets his aid check. Remember, over the year he has borrowed a lot of money from you and has never paid you back. You even tried to get him a new job with your company and he said he didn't want it. What do you tell him, looking him straight in the face? That you think he's a bum and no, he will get no more free rides from you? Do you tell him you love

38

him with the love of the Lord but you can't do that anymore? Tell him you think he's using the money you gave him for drugs? Just look at him and walk away? Remind him that he could have had a good job at the post office, and if he didn't want it that was his problem? Just hand him the money, walk away, smile, and pray? Or tell him you have three dependent children already and you can't support another person? You decide what you would do.

The Tragedy and the Blessing

—■—

Imagine that you are a married man and you and your wife are born again Christians. The marriage is a beautiful one and you know that the Lord has placed your wife in your life. After you are married for about two years, the Lord blesses both of you with a little girl. Your daughter is so beautiful that you love her as much or even more than your wife, because you know that she is a gift from God. One day while coming home from work you find your wife lying on the couch looking as though she's fast asleep. You go over to wake her up and you get no response. Immediately you dial 911 for an ambulance and also a Christian friend to watch the baby while you go to the hospital with your wife.

Within a few minutes the ambulance arrives, and your Christian friend shortly thereafter. You tell your friend the whole story. Your wife is being transported to the nearest hospital and you ride with her in the ambulance. While in route to the hospital your wife stops breathing and there is nothing else the paramedics can do for her. She is pronounced D.O.A. (dead on arrival), the cause being an apparent heart attack. All that time you were praying for your wife, but the Lord took her home with Him. You begin to cry and all through the funeral you cry.

Even weeks after the funeral you are still crying over the death of your wife because you loved her so much. Then one night the Lord speaks to you in a dream and says your wife is with Him now because her work was finished. He also tells you to stop crying and raise your little daughter to glorify Him. You wake up happy because your wife made it into heaven and the Lord spoke to you for the first time. You go on with your normal life, raising your daughter and teaching her about Jesus Christ.

Years have gone by and your daughter is now twelve and she get cramps. There is also a little spot of blood in her panties. She comes to you with the problem and tells you her symptoms. Immediately you know that her period or monthly is about to start. What do you do? Remember that you have never remarried. Do you run to the library to get a book on the subject, or ask one of the many women that you associate with to explain it to your daughter? Do you pray first for guidance and tell her as simply as you can that all females go through this process once a month, that it's the first change from childhood to womanhood? Or do you let her just learn from the street and forget about the matter? Tell me, what would you do?

April Fools

———◼———

Say that you're a good Christian woman and you are born again, spirit-filled, and speaking in tongues. You have lived a very good Christian life, and everyone that you meet likes you. You also have a very good job as a secretary downtown.

It's the first of April, and everyone knows it's April Fools Day. Ever since you awoke this morning people have been playing tricks on you. Even your husband, who is not saved, and the children have been playing tricks on you.

You have fallen for their tricks every time. So you propose in your mind that no one will ever fool you again for the rest of the day. Well the day goes on and your husband and children are off to work and school. It's time for you to go to work at your part-time job. You're a little tired because you had to cook the meals and get the children off to school, but you're ready for work.

While walking down the street you notice how bright and sunny the day is, and you thank the Lord. In the back of your mind you remember it's April Fools Day and think of how your family tricked you this morning.

When you finally arrive at the bus stop there is a lady standing there that you have seen a few times before in the neighborhood. She comes up beside you. You stand there for a few minutes until see the bus coming from a distance. Immediately you reach into your purse to get your bus pass and drop a twenty dollar bill on the ground.

The lady standing next to you bends down and picks it up. She says, "You dropped this on the ground." Almost instantly you smile and say, "I know it's April Fools Day and you can't fool me that easy." The bus arrives; you and the lady get on. All the while she's trying to explain that the money is yours. You say that you're not a fool for anyone and walk to the back of the bus to get away from her.

Meanwhile, the rest of the passengers overhear the conversation and tell the lady, "If she doesn't believe you, keep it for yourself." The lady tries once more to give you the twenty dollars, but you won't listen. So the lady puts the bill in her pocket and walks away. Later at work you begin going through your purse and discover that the money was yours. You begin to cry because you have just been fooled again, but this time by yourself.

The next day you see the same lady at the bus stop. She tells you thanks for the twenty dollars, it came in handy for a birthday gift for her son. Now what do you say and do? Tell the lady you want your money back? Smile and say, "Praise the Lord, the money was a blessing to someone"? Beat the lady up and take the little money she has left? Decide not to say anything because you were the fool on April Fools? You tell me, what would you do?

The Newlyweds

———■———

Suppose that you are a young, beautiful Christian woman in your mid twenties. You have been living on your own since you were eighteen years old. You have been faithful in your walk with Jesus in the three years since your born again experience. You have been attending a good church where you sing in the choir. For the last year and a half you have come to know many different young people at the church and in choir rehearsals. All the people you have met have different and refreshing personalities and you like them all. Some have even become very close friends of yours. You have a closer attachment to one particular young man by the name of Greg.

You and Greg have been seeing each other (no sex) for the last year. You go out to the movies, parks, Christian outings, and rehearsals together. Greg is twenty-eight years old, three years older than you are. He has always been a Christian gentlemen whenever you go out to sing or talk to each other. Greg has never made advances toward you. He's always been a gentlemen and you know he loves God because his conversations center around Jesus. Also, he has the Holy Spirit within him and the joys of the Lord just beam from him. You have come to know Greg very well; you also have come to love him, but you try to keep it from him and put your mind more on the Lord.

Well, one day out of the blue Greg says that he loves you and would like you to become his wife. You're surprised because you didn't think Greg felt the same way about you that you do about him. So you pray about it and believe in your heart that this is the man for you. You and Greg set a wedding date six months from the day he asked you. Within the next six months Greg tells you more and more about his family life and background. You feel Greg is very open and honest about his strong relationship with God and family. But you are very closed mouth about your family relationships, especially your relationships with your mother and father. You only say that you grew up and moved out at eighteen and that you love Jesus.

The six months pass very quickly and the wedding date has arrived. Greg wants to get married at the church and you agree with him. Greg asks if your mother and father are coming to the wedding, and you lie and say that they're out of town on emergency family business. So Greg's father stands in for your dad to give the bride away.

An hour later you and Greg become husband and wife. Then you begin your honeymoon at one of the most exclusive hotels in the city. The hotel suite is beautiful and Greg and you prepare for bed. OK, Greg is ready in 12.8 seconds and he is waiting for you. You're still in the washroom getting ready.

After a while Greg becomes worried about you and asks if you are all right. You says yes and come out with tears in your eyes. He asks you what is the matter, and you sit beside him on the bed. After a few minutes of silence you speak in a shaky voice. You tell him that your parents aren't really out of town on family business. You just didn't tell them about the wedding because you didn't want them to come. You go on to say that at the age of twelve that your father molested you and you never told anyone. You say you've tried to tell your mother, but she didn't want to hear it. She just closed herself off from you. You say you've hated your mom and dad for years and that you have drifted further apart. You add that you have blocked it out of your memory for all of these years, but your honeymoon night brought it back to the surface. You tell your husband that long after that you felt dirty and unclean and you just wanted to die after that night. You scream out with a loud voice that you love your husband, but you can't go through with the honeymoon. You and your husband both cry.

As this young lady's husband, what do you do? Begin praying and laying hands on her for deliverance? Think about it for a while and then get a divorce? Go kill her father for doing this to a young child—your wife? Seek good Christian counseling for your wife and for yourself because your wife is a victim of incest? What would you do?

The Game

———————■———————

Suppose you're a young woman, a Christian about fifteen years old. You're still living with your mother and father, who have raised you to love Jesus Christ as your Lord and Saviour. You have a wonderful family life and even more beautiful prayer life with Jesus. You attend church every time the doors open. The church you attend has a youth group that meets the third Saturday of every month and you attend regularly. For the last year you have come to know all the teenagers that go to the youth meetings. There is one boy in particular that you have come to know and like very well, and his name is Issac. Issac is a very good looking teenager and he is a year older than you.

After some time, you and Issac feel that you like each other, so you start dating. At first you start going to the movies, then Christian concerts and Bible study meetings together. But you still haven't told your mom and dad that you're dating Issac. You and Issac have been kissing and hugging and getting closer to each other. Then one day while you and Issac are on a date, Issac looks at you point blank and says that he loves you very much and you're the only girl for him. He also says he wants a closer relationship with you. He tells you that he wants to make love to you, and that if you want the relationship to go any further you should feel the same way. Issac says he'll give you a few days to think about having sex with him or lose him forever. He takes you home so you can sleep on his proposal.

The next day you awake, greeting your mom and dad half heartedly, and prepare for school. Your mom notices something is troubling you and asks you what is the problem. You look at her, wanting to tell her about Issac and his wanting to sleep with you, but you say nothing is wrong and go off to school. When you arrive at school you see some of your non-Christian classmates and begin to ask them questions about sex. You ask how it feels, how you do it, and are you changed afterwards—questions of that nature. One girl named Janice speaks right up without hesitation and says, "Girl there is nothing like having sex to make you feel like a real woman. I have been having sex ever since I was twelve years old and I love it, and can't do without it. Anyway, if you don't have sex by the age of seventeen you'll probably go blind or crazy. Anyway, every girl I know is doing it. You mean you are still a virgin?" She walks away laughing at you. One of the girls you were talking to says, "If you want to do it the right way, here's the name and address of a free clinic. They'll give you all the free birth control pills you need." So you decide to visit the clinic to be at least prepared just in case you and Issac do sleep together.

That evening after school you stop by the clinic, along the way you can't help thinking about Janice and how she laughed at you, and that all the girls are having sex and you must be the last virgin on earth.

You go inside the clinic and the lady at the desk asks if she can help you. You're speechless and at a loss for words, but manage to tell the lady you're there for some birth control pills. She looks at you, smiles, and says, "Sign this simple form that your parents won't be notified and that you're making a very wise decision." The doctor comes out to examine you and gives you a two-month supply of birth control pills. He also says that whenever you need some more you should just come in and pick them up. You walk away a little confused because you thought it would be harder than that to get contraceptives.

You hurry home, being very careful to put your birth control pills in a safe place. A few days pass and Issac asks you again about having sex with him. You reluctantly say yes to keep him as your boyfriend. Issac says that there is no one at his home, that his parents will be gone all night. So you call your parents and lie, saying that you'll be home a little late because you're over at a girlfriend's house studying for an exam tomorrow at school. Your parents trust you, because you never have lied to them before. You say you'll be home by 10:00 p.m. and that you will see them later.

When you reached Issac's house, he can't wait to get your clothes off, but you let him do what he wants and it's slam, bam, thank you ma'am. Issac is happy and proud that he has now slept with you and considers himself a man now. But you feel that you have gone against everything you and your parents believe in and that you turned your back on Jesus. You arrive home at 9:45, tell your mother that you're tired, and say good night. When you get to bed you cry softly all night and drift off to sleep because of what you have done.

Two weeks pass and you an Issac are still dating. Then one day he takes you out and tells you that he has fallen out of love with you and that it was fun while it lasted. He says that he has found someone new and doesn't want to be around you anymore. You run home crying your heart out because you thought he loved you and your love would last forever. When you arrive home you hide your hurt and shame from your family. You go straight to your room, telling your mom you're not hungry and you had a burger and fries earlier. So she says OK and doesn't bother you.

Weeks pass and you haven't seen or heard from Issac, not even at church. It's Sunday and you and your family are preparing for church. You're in the bathroom getting ready. While you are in there washing up, your mother enters your room to borrow some deodorant because she has just run out. While going through your dresser drawer she comes across the birth control pills you got from the clinic weeks before. She waits for you to finish washing up.

When you get to your room she confronts you with the pills in her hands and asks why you have them. You are surprised, shocked, and don't know what to say. So what do you do from here on? Lie and say you're keeping them for a friend? Tell her you found them outside? Tell her you thought they were candy? Or tell her the whole story from beginning to end—sex and everything? What do you do?

Monkey See Monkey Do

———■———

Suppose that you are a Christian in your thirties. You weren't always a Christian, however, so let's say you were recently born again, within the last year. You are also married with a son about thirteen years old, and when you got married you and your wife were sinners. I mean you lived life as the chief of sinners, but you grew tired of the party life, the dope scene, and cheating on your wife. So one day a male Christian witnessed to you and you accepted Jesus Christ as your Lord and Saviour, because deep in your heart you were ready for the Lord. You started attending church, going to Bible study, and forming a deeper relationship with Jesus.

One day you try witnessing to your son and wife. They believe and accept what you say and start attending church services with you. But then your wife says that she has a lot of living to do and that you have turned into one of those Christian fanatics. She also says that you should live your life, she should live hers, and for you to leave her alone. So you don't pressure her with the issue of coming to Christ and giving up all of her sins, but you say that you love her very much and that you will keep praying for her. All she does is laugh softly and walk away.

Well, Wednesday rolls around and it's time for Wednesday evening services at the church. You arrive home a little early from work to eat dinner and you and your son prepare for worship service. While you are dressing, your wife is also dressing to go out to a party.

51

You ask her where she is going. She says she is going out with the girls and will be back when she is good and ready. You want to grab her by her throat and tell her that she is not going anywhere, but you refrain from doing and saying what is on your mind. You tell her to have a good time with the girls.

You and your son arrive at church and you listen to a very good sermon by the pastor on forgiveness of sins. The sermon is so good that your son and you stand up and praise the Lord at the completion of the services.

Meanwhile, your wife is at the party living it up like life has no end. She is drinking, smoking dope, and even snorting a little cocaine. She is higher than a Georgia pine and she doesn't even know what time it is. While she is enjoying herself, a man walks over and starts talking to her. After a while they leave together to go to his place for further drinks and dancing.

Eventually they end up in bed together, having sex. You and your son make it home about 12:00 midnight and you start wondering what your wife could be doing this late at night. So you make a few calls to her friends. One of the girlfriends she went to the party with lies to you by telling you she got a little high tonight and she is spending the night with her. Then she says you can't talk to her because she is asleep on the couch and she says for you not to worry. So you don't worry about your wife, but go to bed praying for her because you have an early day at work tomorrow.

While you are sleeping, the Lord deals with you in a dream and he shows you exactly where and with whom your wife is. So 8:00 a.m. comes around and your wife still hasn't come home. Then you decide to call out that day and call your wife's friend back. You tell her you know exactly where your wife is and hang up the phone. Well, your wife strolls in about 8:30 and she is crying. You tell her you know where she has been and what she has been doing all night long. Your wife begins crying even harder

52

than before and tries to explain what happened. She goes on to say that she didn't know what she was doing and thought it was all a dream. Also, she falls on her knees, asks that you forgive her, and promises that it will never happen again. She says that you are right, Jesus is the only answer to salvation. Well, after hearing her confession you get mad and want to use her head for a dust mop to clean the whole house. However, you know it is nothing but the devil placing these thoughts in your head.

Tell me what would you do, keeping in mind the beautiful sermon the pastor gave on forgiveness last night. Tell me, would you beat your wife for her transgressions? Or would you blackmail your wife for the rest of her life if she ever got out of line again? Would you stone your wife for her inequities as in the Old Testament? Would you forgive your wife because you realize that Christ forgave you for your sins, and as you are walking in love begin to minister to her from John 3:16? Or would you seek Christian counseling?

The Brothers

———————■———————

I have a friend by the name of Bob. He is about thirty-five years old, married with four children. The youngest child is three years old. His wife is also thirty-five years old. Both are Christians and are saved. Bob loves his wife, Chris, very much and spends as much time with the children as his time and schedule will permit him when he's not at work. Bob is a factory worker for General Foods on the south side of the city. Most of the time, when he is not at work or with the wife and kids, he's at church. He attends a very good church, he likes the pastor, and loves the Lord Jesus Christ. Before Bob got married he spent a lot of his time with his family at home. He would go to work and return back home. Bob had very strong family ties, even though they didn't get along that well before he was saved.

Well, when he got saved things started to change around his home. He loved his mother more than his brother and sister. They didn't know how to show love to one another. Well, in the middle of his marriage of five years the Lord, through Bob, ministers salvation to his mother and she receives Jesus and is saved. But things still aren't easy around the house, and he still lets his light shine for Jesus. So shortly after the prayer of salvation for his mother, she goes home to live with the Lord. Well, the death of Bob's mother shakes him a great deal, but the Lord reassures him, in his heart that his mother is with Him now and he should go on living for Him. The death of his mother brought on a deeper relationship with his brother Calvin. Now Calvin isn't saved, but Bob loves him anyway. Well, months later after the passing of his mom Bob moves out to live with his wife. Before that time he was taking care of his mother, a stroke and heart attack victim, and during that time he was spending most of the time with his mother and his wife. His wife didn't understand the family relationship or the reason why they couldn't be together all the time.

But he loved his mother and he knew that she needed him to take care of her. His wife could have moved in with him, but because of her own family problems it was impossible. Bob knew what the word said, that when a man gets married he should leave his mother and father and cleave unto his wife, and when a man finds a wife, he finds a good thing. He also knew that he had to take care of his mother because she took care of him as a child. He wanted to return that loving care.

Back to the brothers. As time goes on they draw closer and closer together. They still argue with one another, but they always come back to each other and apologize for what they said to each other. Bob's wife really doesn't understand this closeness of the brothers, and one day she confronts him about the issue. She says she doesn't like him spending all his spare time with his brother and for him to stop seeing Calvin and start spending all that extra time with her. Well, Bob said he would start to spend a little more time with her and did. But he kept on seeing his brother whenever he could. Bob's wife still didn't like the situation. She confronted him again and said straight out, "If you don't stop seeing your brother you can say good-bye to our relationship."

You, being a Christian, tell me what would you do in a situation like this? Would you tell your wife, "I love you honey, but I also love my brother, so if you want to leave I can't stop you"? Would you tell her to stop being jealous of your brother and buy her some flowers? Would you take her out to dinner to reassure her of your love for her? Or would you seek Christian counseling on the matter? Tell me, what would you do?

Life and Death

———— ■ ————

I have a friend named Kristy McCallum and she is my very best friend. We share almost everything together, except religious practices. The reason I said what I did is because I am a Christian and Kristy, well she has her doubts, but we are still friends. Kristy and I came from the same hometown of South Holland, Connecticut with its population of 30,000 and still growing. In our neighborhood everyone knew each other and cared about each other. We lived on Hillary Street and our homes were right across the street from our church, The Morning Star Christian Church, which I attend every Sunday morning and sometimes during the week. Kristy and I went to Maple Leaf Elementary School. As children we played and fought together, but deep down we loved each other like sisters. As we begin to grow up Kristy and I attended the high school across town because our neighborhood didn't have a high school. In high school Kristy was still the same as in grade school, making the straight As, overly friendly and popular, but I was the shy one with a C average. During high school Kristy and I started to put some distance between us. She started to call me once a month just to tell me what was happening with her. Every now and then, between Kristy's talking so much, I was able to witness to her a little about Jesus. But the majority of the time, when Kristy didn't call at her usual time, I would just pray for her. One day Kristy gave me the strange call. She was depressed about some boy named Phillip

Baker that had dumped her. Now she was expecting a baby because she moved too quickly too soon. Then she started crying because she overheard some girls talking in the girls washroom about an abortion clinic. She wanted me to go with her there to have an abortion.

Tell me what you would do if you were in my place? Would you take her to the abortion clinic? Would you tell her mother? Would you tell her that abortion is murder and show her in the Word?

Mail Order Bride

————■————

Mr. James Gregory is another example of a famous black soldier of war. He served in the war in Vietnam for two years during the 1960s. James had just turned fifty years old and he praised the Lord everyday for allowing him to live that long. There were many times when he thought he wouldn't make it. For example, when James was stationed in Fort Dobbs in Missouri, he was in charge of the demolition equipment. He and some of the men had just come from some practice testing of new equipment that had arrived the day before when he stopped the men from accidently stepping into a mine field that had been left behind by the Viet Cong. Because of his bravery he received not only a Congressional Medal of Honor for bravery, but also a promotion in rank to Lieutenant James Gregory. Afterward, Lieutenant Gregory returned home to the place where he was not only born but also where he was raised. James was from Nantucket, Kentucky, not far from Louisville. He had a big four bedroom, red brick home surrounded by a white picket fence. James' home was on Seventh and Peach Streets. The neighborhood was nice and clean and all the neighbors loved and respected him because he was a military man.

The neighborhood that James lived in had a little church down the street called New Testament Christian Temple where James worshipped often. James was a Christian and he had received Christ during his time in the army. James had seen the Lord bring him through many dangers while he was there. The Lord had blessed James with a very good job. He got a chance to go to college and earn a degree in electrical engineering while he was stationed in the service. Now he was receiving the fruit of his labor because of it. James worked for Flaxston Electronics Company, and because of his degree and training in this particular area, he earned a cool 1,000 dollars a week. When he left work he would usually go straight to the bowling alley where he was in a league. James' bowling average was 300 because he practiced as often as he could

Despite all his busy activities and the job, James felt there was always something missing. James was never much on dating because he was naturally a shy guy. In his church he had tried to befriend some of the women, but they got the wrong impression about him so he left them alone.

As the days passed by, James became more lonely and impatient. During his quiet time he would talk to the Lord about needing a wife by his side to share in his life. As always there was no response from above. So James decided to give God some help. James had always been impulsive and when things didn't move fast enough for him, he would make them move. The other day when he was throwing out some junk mail a particular magazine caught his eye. So he took the magazine out of the garbage can and began to thumb through it. Lo and behold a certain ad caught his attention. He read the ad out of the old *Cosmo* magazine which he had almost thrown away: "Mail order brides by the 1000s from different states and countries, take your pick for a cool fee of $500 down." As he continued to read the ad he struggled with himself about whether he would be able to make the right decision. He prayed and believed God was guiding him.

Now tell me what would you do in this situation? Order the bride and believe God was guiding you? Get involved in computer dating? Blind dating? Become a monk and go into the monastery? Let the church match you up? What? You tell me.

The Ultimatum

■

Imagine that you are a husband and wife in the Lord. You have four children and you and your wife have been saved for five years. Also, you knew your wife for sixteen years before you got married. Before you got married both of you loved the Lord with all your hearts and souls. Plus you attend a very good church on the south side of Chicago that seats five thousand people. The pastor knows and lives the Word daily and you love your new Christian home.

Well, before you got married you and your wife had good jobs. Your wife worked at the main post office as a mail handler and you worked for a major company in the city as a janitor making good money. You and your wife were happy that you both decided to get married. Both of you praised the Lord and looked forward to the future together. I mean that even on your off days you told your hopes and dreams to one another. Your wife told you she wanted to be a Christian nurse, and you wanted to be a Christian billionaire. Each day you prayed for each other's desire to do a work for the Lord and support your family.

OK, shortly after you get married both of you lose your jobs. However, you go on praising the Lord and giving thanks for what you do have. Then your wife is reduced to going on public aid and you are still trying to find work of any kind. Months go by and you finally find work with a temporary agency. The work is good, but the jobs are few and far between. Now remember, during all this time you still have been attending church services and paying your tithes like clock work.

Years go by and you and your wife are still in the same situation—no jobs and public aid. I mean the situation is so bad that you can't even afford new clothes to attend church on Sundays. All the clothes that you and your children wear are given to you from the members at the church. Now you are thinking of going back into the world and considering the way they do things, because you always had a job before you got saved. So you stop going to church so much because you are becoming more and more discouraged. This is not because of pride, but because you hear all the beautiful testimonies of people being blessed by the Lord. This is very wonderful for other people and you don't put it down, but you begin to feel that you are doing something wrong and the Lord is not hearing your prayers. Well, four years have passed and the same situation exists with you, your wife, and family.

One day your wife comes up to you and gives you an ultimatum. She says that she's very discouraged and that there must be sin in your lives. "Maybe," she says, "the Lord didn't want us to get married." She also states that if things don't change within the next few months, she will take the kids and leave. She will get a divorce from you, she says, then she turns and walks away. Well, you're not surprised because she has been complaining for some time now. You as a man understand how she feels and begin to look even harder for a job, and you even pray harder.

The time your wife stated has almost come and by now you have stopped paying tithes, but your wife continues to do so. Now you and your wife are both discouraged. You're just hanging on with a mustard seed of faith. Tell me what would you do in a situation like this? Believe there is sin in your lives and go get deliverance? Believe that you and your wife were not meant to marry in the first place? Pray and seek the Lord even harder for an answer? Seek Christian counseling at your church? Or just let your wife get the divorce that has been on her mind? You tell me what would you do?

The Troubled Teen

———■———

I once had a friend by the name of Mary. Mary was not saved and was not a Christian, but she was a very beautiful person inside as well as outside. She had an inner beauty that could only be surpassed by God's presence and God's love. Mary was eighteen and about five feet seven inches tall, very shapely, with an outgoing personality. I watched her grow up as a child, and I was about ten years older than she. Whenever I saw her, she had only nice things to say. I mean, it could be the worst day of the year and Mary would say, "Isn't it a beautiful day?" and smile.

However, Mary had one draw back in her life, and that was when she reached eighteen she thought she was a grown woman. She was still a virgin at eighteen and there's nothing wrong with being a virgin at eighteen, or even at forty years old. Well anyway, all the young teenage boys wanted to sleep with her—not because she was beautiful, only because she was a challenge for them. The only thing she would do on school days was go home and study. On the weekends she would go out and party. And this is where all her problems began.

Her mother would try to tell her that most of the boys she was seeing were no good for her. That all the young boys wanted with her was to knock her up and ruin her education. One night Mary went out to a party with a young boy on the south side of Chicago (back then we used to call them house sets). Mary was enjoying herself at the party, drinking a little and dancing. Then she made one mistake, she got a can of pop, drank half, and laid the half empty can next to her date and went to the ladies room. While she was gone, unknown to her, her date slipped a pill in her drink and stirred it before she returned. The pill dropped in her drink was PCP. Mary returned and finished her drink, because she trusted the boy that she was with.

After she finished the pop she asked her date for another dance. While dancing she began to feel strange and very peculiar. Then she asked the boy to take her home. It was late, about 11:30 p.m. She began to stagger and fall, but the boy managed to put her in the back seat of his car and drive off. Instead of driving her home, he drove to a very secluded, quiet area of the city. By this time Mary didn't know up from down. The young boy began taking her clothes off and began having sex with her. After laying with her, he put her clothes on and drove her home.

He left her on the stairs, rang the bell, and took off in his car without anyone seeing him. The boy was never heard from again. Well, Mary's mother came to the door, found her in a daze and called the doctor. The doctor said that Mary has taken some kind of dope and should be all right in a couple of days. But Mary was never fine after that day. She kept remembering bits and pieces of that night in the back seat of that car.

When Mary returned to school the whole school was talking about her having sex in the back seat of the young boy's car. Mary was ashamed and hurt, and she was still not thinking straight because the drugs had messed up her mind. So she began talking out of her head, saying that she wanted to die. She even talked to me as a friend that watched her grow up. But I wasn't a Christian at that time, and I joked it off and walked away. Her mother took her very seriously, though, and drove her to the hospital again. Mary was examined and they couldn't find anything wrong with her. They sent her home. About two weeks later, Mary began talking about suicide again. She said she had just taken a bottle of sleeping pills, and she was very serious this time. But no one believed her and her mother sent her upstairs to her room. An hour passed and we were all sitting in the living room talking when we hear a loud noise hit the floor. We all ran upstairs to see what all the commotion was about and we found Mary face down on the floor with an empty bottle of sleeping pills in her hand. Her mother dialed 911 and called for an ambulance, but it was too late. Mary died from an overdose of sleeping pills.

Now everyone is sorry that they didn't believe her threat of suicide. But being sorry won't bring Mary back. Tell me what would you have done in this situation, being a Christian? Prayed for Mary and sought counseling for her? Believed Mary's threat of suicide and watched her carefully? If Mary was your daughter, would you have killed the boy who did this to her? You tell me what you would have done? Sometimes I still carry the guilt around with me to this day. Please forgive me Mary.

In Confidence

———■———

I once had a Christian friend by the name of Bob. He was married to his wife, Chris, for over five years. Bob and Chris were Christians and had a growing family of four children. They had a somewhat happy marriage. Well one day Bob decided to trust his life story to his wife Chris. I mean he told her almost every detail of his life, things that he had never told or spoken of to anyone except Jesus before. He told her about smoking dope, getting over an illness in his life, and many other personal stories. He also told her many of the unclean things he had done when he was not saved. Bob considered his wife his best friend and someone he could trust.

Well, weeks and even months went by after Bob told his story to his wife Chris. Then things started to go bad in the finances of the family. Bob lost his job and was looking for any type of work to support his family. Then Chris started feeling that God had abandoned her and the family. She started confiding in one of her friends by the name of Shirley, a Christian evangelist. Shirley was not a counselor but just a close friend that Chris grew up with. Chris began to tell Shirley everything that Bob had trusted her with. I mean everything he had confided in her a few months earlier. Now remember, Bob is now saved but still is working things out in his life. Shirley told Chris that the Lord didn't put her and her husband Bob together and that maybe she should consider getting out of the marriage altogether. Shirley, her friend, is married to a nice guy.

Later in the month Bob came in contact with Shirley at church. Without knowing that this conversation went on between his wife and Shirley, Bob went over to say hello, but Shirley just rolled her eyes and walked away from Bob. Bob didn't think anything of it and went on enjoying the services. This went on for a while and Bob began to wonder what was going on with Shirley, and also with his wife Chris. Then Chris told Bob that she told Shirley everything about what Bob had told her in confidence. Well, Bob got very upset and angry with his wife, but he managed to ask her a question or two. Bob asked Chris why she told Shirley all of his business, and if she took up for him when Shirley said that they shouldn't be together as husband and wife. Then Chris looked down and said no she didn't. Now Bob was even madder at Chris than ever before because she didn't take up for him with her friend Shirley. He considered Chris his best friend and she let him down.

Well, it took Bob about a week to let go of the anger that he had for Shirley and, especially, for his wife. He slowly remembered the words of the Lord, to "be angry, but sin not." After that Bob never trusted his wife with anything important again. He knew if the marriage lasted it would take Chris a long time to regain his trust.

Men, as a Christian married or single man, tell me what would you do in a situation like this? Get the divorce that her friend Shirley suggested? Just pray for your wife because anyone can make a mistake? Never tell your wife anything personal again? Be a little more circumspect about what you say to your wife from now on? Take your wife on a long trip and drop her off a bridge somewhere? Brothers, tell me exactly what would you do?

Looks Can Be Deceiving

———■———

My story begins in the year 1989. It is a very warm summer. This story focuses on a young Christian man by the name of Albert. Albert is about thirty years old and very much in love with the Lord Jesus Christ. Albert is single and works as an air traffic controller at O'Hare Airport. He's been working at this job for the last three years. Albert, who has been saved for the last five years, has an outgoing personality. He loves being around people and helping anyone he can.

One day his boss asks him if he would mind switching jobs for just one day and work as a transporter. A transporter is a person who transports people from the airplane to the airline terminal or station. Albert doesn't mind at all because it would be a delightful change from his regular routine. He agrees with a smile and hurries down to report to his new job. The first plane load of people arrives and Albert greets them with a smile and asks them how they enjoyed their flight. They all say it was wonderful and ask him his name. When they reach the terminal they give the airline nothing but praise for hiring a good employee such as Albert.

Well, with the second flight of people the same thing happens and Albert is floating on cloud nine. Now the third flight arrives and Albert is loading the people into his van when he notices one of the most beautiful women he has ever seen in his life. Albert can't resist saying hello to her and asks her personally how she enjoyed her flight to Chicago. She say, "Very well, thank you." She seems to like Albert's concern for her and she sits up front, close to Albert. Then she and Albert get into a deeper conversation. She tells Albert that her name is Shirley and she just arrived from California because her company needed a new advertising manager here in Chicago. She reveals that she is twenty-eight years old. Albert says that is wonderful and tells her about his job as an air traffic controller. He also says that he is very happy that he had a chance to do the transporter's job today because he wouldn't have met her. She smiles.

Albert goes on further to say that he's a Christian and invites her to his church. He gives her the address to the church, his full name, and telephone number. Then he leaves and tells her to have a God-blessed rainbow day. He says he'll be looking forward to seeing her at his church.

Weeks go by and Albert can't stop thinking about Shirley, about how beautiful she was and how good their conversation was. Then a month passes and Albert is at Sunday service enjoying the message when all of a sudden he turns around, looks at the door, and sees Shirley. Shirley sees him and sits next to him. Albert says hello with a great big smile. His smile is so wide that you would have thought he was related to jaws. Well after the service, Shirley and Albert go out to dinner and talk a lot more about their jobs and themselves.

Shirley says she would have gotten in touch with him sooner, but she has been so busy in the last few weeks. Albert smiles and says, "That's all right. Don't worry about it." So they finish dinner and Albert takes her home. During the next four months Albert and Shirley begin seeing a lot of each other at church, movies, and dinners. In those four months Shirley attends Albert's church and goes up for salvation. Now Albert begins thinking maybe Shirley is the woman for him and entertains the thought of marriage to Shirley. Within the next few months he asks her for her hand in marriage and marries her.

After Albert and Shirley are married for about a year, Shirley comes to him and says she has a secret to tell him. She tells Albert to sit down and be very quiet—and please don't get angry. Shirley tells Albert that she is a transsexual, that years ago she was a man but was very unhappy with that lifestyle and had a sex change operation to become a woman for good. She also says she is very sorry for lying to him and for not telling him the truth. Well, the big smile on Albert's face slowly begins to turn into a frown and Albert begins to realize that he is in big trouble. He has stepped out of the will of God. Tell me what you would do if you were Albert? Get a divorce and run to the church and repent for your sins? Kill Shirley for deceiving you in your relationship? Go get yourself Christian counseling? You tell me.

Schizoid Christian

———————————■———————————

This is a story about a man that I once knew by the name of James. James had a very unhappy childhood. He was the first-born of four children and he was a very light-skinned Negro growing up in the mid-fifties on the west side of Chicago. The only one that really loved James was his father, who worked as a janitor downtown. Whenever his dad had any free time, he would dress James up and take him out to places like Riverview, or they would just to go get a burger or something. He would spend as much time with James as he could. James' mother didn't like him that much and his brother and sister would tease him about being so light-skinned. When they would go to school they would run off and leave James by himself. In fact, this happened whenever they would go anywhere together.

Then the teasing would continue from his brother and sister at school and at home whenever they were around school friends. They would say things like, "We have a white boy in our family and he thinks that he is better than us. Come on an see our white brother." James' brother and sister would even charge admission for people to see their white brother. This would make James very angry, but he would just forget it go out and play by himself.

Well, when James was about nine years old tragedy struck his family. One day Doris, James' mother, sent him and his two brothers and sister over to a friend's house about three blocks away, by themselves. Doris figured that because James was the oldest he could be trusted with the responsibility of watching the other children.

So . . . James and his brothers and sister are off to Pearl's house, Doris' close friend. On the way out Mike, James' brother who is eight years old, says he wants to take their puppy along with them. They all are on their way, the puppy too, walking down the street and come to an intersection. James looks both ways and they cross the street. They are half way to Pearl's house now and her house is on the other side of the street. Instead of crossing the street at the corner they decide to cross the street between two parked cars. While James is holding on to his youngest brother Leon he hears a car racing down the street in their direction. Just then the puppy breaks free and runs across the street. James', brother and sister, Mike and Gloria run behind the puppy to the other side. Within a fraction of a second, Leon who is six years old, breaks free from James and runs into the middle of the street, but he doesn't make it all the way across before the car, driven by a drunken driver, slams into Leon and throws him into the air about sixty feet. Leon is dead before he even hits the ground. Blood is coming out of his forehead and he's just laying in the street.

James is paralyzed with fear and can't move; he's in a daze. He looks at his brother in the street, lifeless, and can hear someone telling him to run back home to get his mother and father, but James does nothing, just stands there staring. So his brother and sister run home and get his mother. Doris, his mother, arrives crying and the ambulance arrives few minutes later. But there's nothing they can do for Leon; he's dead. The driver that ran into Leon is charged with driving under the influence and he has his license suspended—that's all.

However, James, two days later, begins to cry and blame himself because he could have run in the street or held his little brother's hand tighter than he did. James cries for weeks with no relief. Then he begins to blame his mother for sending him and his brother out that day. James also blames his other brother and sister, because if they had not run across the street after the puppy, Leon wouldn't have chased behind them and he would still be alive.

So James learns how to hate at an early age, but his mother isn't very concerned and believes that James will be all right in time. James doesn't really gets over his hate and anger though. He just hides it and eventually it looks as though everything is all right because his father explains things to him and reassures him everything will be fine. A couple of years pass by and tragedy strikes James' family again. James' father, the one he loves so much, dies of internal bleeding from a fight at work. Now James is very unhappy and sad because he knows that there's no one who loves him and no one he can really talk to about his problems now.

He draws within himself and trusts no one other than himself. James' family eventually moves to the south side of Chicago and settles around 45th Street. Life becomes a little easier for James and his family, but James is always a problem student in school. He makes friends with some of the other problem preteens in the area and starts staying out late at night. Doris, his mother, really doesn't know this because she has to work evenings and James makes it in just before she comes home.

While associating with other teenagers one night James and the boys decided to break into their public school. James climbs up to a window, aided by his friends, using their bodies as a human latter. He breaks the window, climbs in, goes around to the front door, and opens it for the rest of the boys.

They all get inside and begin to vandalize the school. They mess up as many classrooms as possible within a short period of time, then leave, taking little things like chalk, crayons, pencils, and pens. One of the boys that James broke into the school with tells his younger brother, who tells the story to his mother. Well, the boys are in trouble and the police are called in. Plus, each boy gets a beating from his parents. After that incident James decides to go straight for a while, but he is still failing in school. They pass him through anyway. By this time James is about thirteen years old and getting into a few fights every now and then. He is basically a loner.

One day after school James is on the back porch playing. His brother and sister and a few other kids are with him. (James lived on the third floor.) The girls are jumping rope and the boys are doing what they do best, teasing the girls. Everything just going along just fine until one of the three girls jumping rope loses control of the rope. It gets tangled up in the electrical wire connected to the building. James runs over and offers to free the rope entangled in the wire, but the eleven-year-old girl says she can do it herself. James says, "All right, do it yourself." The girl climbs over the railing and James is next to her. She reaches the rope and just then loses her balance and falls straight down. James watches her fall. She hits her head on three concrete stairs and dies instantly.

All the parents are aroused by the noise and come running. The mother of the little girl runs to the railing and begins crying. James is also crying because once again he's in a helpless situation and can't do anything about it. It reminds James of his little brother Leon who died years earlier. It takes weeks for James to get over this tragedy, but he recovers.

Six months pass and the incident is almost forgotten by everyone except James who is thirteen and one half years old and still wetting the bed and having nightmares about that awful day.

Well, to make a long story short, within the next ten years James sees the death of two other people—one suicide and the other a murder between a woman and her husband. James also gets shot in the leg and stabbed in the back. He witnesses the rape of his mother Doris and learns about masturbation and drugs. After all this James winds up in the mental institution for five months and witnesses more atrocities against the patients. He returns home more mixed up than before. He gets involved in pornography and occult practices that he learned from watching TV. This lasts for another six months and James returns to Tinley Park Mental Institution. He stays for another three months and returns home to his family again.

By this time he is worn out by all the things that have happened in his life and he begins to watch religious programs. One day he cries out to the Lord to save his life. Almost instantly he receives the Lord and the Gift of Salvation. He repents for all the things he has done in his life. James has not been institutionalized in three years and Jesus has taken all of the pain away in his life.

Now James reaches the age of twenty-six and his mother, Doris, has had a stroke. James takes care of her while his brother and sister, Mike and Gloria, leave home and give him all the pressures of taking care of their mom. The pressure is great on James, but Jesus has entered into his life and all of the hate he had for his mother and family has now turned into love. He takes care of his mother and finds a beautiful wife and gets married, but his time is split between his wife and his mother. Eventually his mother dies of heart failure in a hospital and James moves in with his wife. All James wants to do is support his new family and keep tender memories of his mother, but because James has been institutionalized, it's hard for him to find good jobs. So he works at any kind of job he can find (temporary work). Life goes on. The End.

Now, tell me what you think of James' story. Tell me what you think of James and his life as a Christian. Tell me what you would do? Amen.

Adoption

---■---

Suppose that you were a Christian couple who has been married for about fifteen years. Your name is Eli and your wife's name is Marian. You and your wife have good jobs, you work as a electronics engineer for a large electronics company on the north side. Your wife Marian works as a registered nurse for a hospital on the north side. You earn 2,000 dollars a month and your wife earns six hundred dollars a week. With that kind of salary you have all that money can buy. Being Christians, you try to attend church as much as your job schedules allow. A majority of the time you have the same off days, so you normally spend one of the three off days attending Sweet Narazene Christian Church. This church is four blocks from your home.

The second off day is spent relaxing with each other. And the final off day is usually for washing, shopping, and watching television. You have been blessed with so much from the Lord. You have a beautiful red brick, seven bedroom home, which is kept up by your housekeeper SiSi when you are at work. Your home is in a very expensive neighborhood. You have three beautiful cars, a black Rolls Royce for after-five purposes, a blue Buick for you, and red Camaro for your wife. You would say you are in the money. You are a great example of a successful black Christian American couple.

Even though it seems like you have everything working for you, there is one thing missing in your marriage. You don't have any children. Your wife's gynecologist, Dr. Wosi, told her five years ago that she could never bear children because of the twisted womb she was born with, but you never really gave up hope. You tried for years new methods such as hormone shots, test tubes, surrogate motherhood, and artificial insemination. They were even pushing you into trying corrective surgery and a second opinion, but nothing seems to work. You have come to the conclusion that maybe your wife wasn't meant to have children naturally, so you begin to pray and seek God's advice about adoption. You have so often said it doesn't make any sense to have all this room in the house and not have a child to share it.

Almost immediately you start searching for the best Christian adoption agency, after you get the go ahead from the Lord. Remember, with your family, money is no problem. You are looking for the best Christian adoption agency that money can buy.

So when it seems all is lost, the last adoption agency catches your attention. You anxiously phone Heavenly Kingdom Christian Adoption Agency to make an appointment for the following week. This would give you enough time to make sure this what God wants you to do. Also this gives you a chance to check out the credibility of the agency. The week rolls past quickly. You and your wife are finally going to the agency to meet a woman of color by the name of Mrs. Moss, who happens to be the social worker and owner of the establishment.

As you walk into the office you are very excited and notice everything around you. Then you are met by a beautiful slim black woman by the name of Mrs. Moss who greets you with a smile. As you are introducing yourselves she tells you step-by-step things that have to take place before you can even see pictures of the type of children they have at the agency. Mrs. Moss begins screening and checking out your backgrounds. This type of process takes a couple of weeks. Mrs. Moss even checks out your neighborhood, finances, friends, and home. She says that she wants to make sure that the child you pick is going to good Christian parents.

There are a lot of agencies that really don't care where they send a child to live, but Mrs. Moss says that she is one person who cares about the child's well being. After everything checks out clean, Mrs. Moss gives you the grand tour of the place from top to bottom. She also shows you pictures of the children they have in the agency. As you are looking over the pictures of all the children, one particular child seems to catch your attention. You begin to inquire about the child—race, age, weight, name, family background, health, appetite, religion.

Mrs. Moss smiles eagerly and begins to tell you something about the child. First, the child's name is India Elish Shalom. She is two years old and she was a Jordanian. She weighs only twenty-five pounds, but has a very good appetite and great bill of health. Mrs. Moss tells you that little India was Moslem and that her mother abandoned her outside a Turkish refugee camp because she couldn't feed her.

Mrs. Moss tells you, also, that India has a winning personality. She tells you how her name came about, because you are curious about the name of the child, where it came from and what it means. Mrs. Moss tells that in her private times at home she often prays for the children and the establishment. One of those times while she was seeking God about some things concerning the place and little India, God dropped the name for the child in her spirit. So Mrs. Moss tells you that you can take the child home in a month. This gives you a chance to go home and have your housekeeper help you prepare the nursery.

The days pass and the day finally arrives. You are so excited about going up to the agency and picking up your little girl to take her to her new home. As the days turn into months and the months change into years you watch little India grow up into a beautiful young lady of Christian character and values. India is one that truly loves Jesus and His Word. India is growing up so quickly. She is now thirteen years old. You have never regretted the day you brought her home to be a part of your family.

Now you are concerned about when to tell her that she was adopted and how to tell her. One day, while you are discussing the matter further in your bedroom, India is getting ready to walk in to kiss you good night. She over hears the discussion and confronts you about it.

What would you do if you were in this situation? Tell her everything? Tell her she heard nothing? Tell her nothing at all? Tell her to go to bed? Tell me what you would do. I would like to know.

Jokes

---■---

Wife: Honey, I just found out they named a city after your head.
Husband: What's that dear?
Wife: Nappy Valley.

Wife: Dear, you know I love you, but sometimes I wish dear season was in.

Wife: They need to make a part two to *Rambo*, starring you, honey, and I got just the title for it. Instead of calling it *Rambo* they can call it *Sambo*.

Wife: Honey, when we got married you were a lean, mean, lover supreme and every girl's dream.
Husband: Really, baby.
Wife: Now you're my worst night mare.

Husband: Baby, I love you, but there's something I have to tell you. Your nose is so big I could drive a Buick through it and still have enough for a couple of freeway off ramps.

Wife: Honey, guess who's coming to dinner tomorrow evening?
Husband: Who, dear?
Wife: My mother, father, and my brother.
Husband: Oh Moe, Larry, and Curly.

Wife: Baby, I need some money to buy a new pair shoes.
Husband: OK, honey. I'll give you the money, but I don't think they make size 20.

Wife: Honey, I need some money to buy a new dress.
Husband: OK, the money's on the dresser, and by the way, baby, tell the tent maker I said hello.

You know you need to lose weight when everyone keeps asking you when the baby is due and you're not pregnant.

God must have some poor saints in the church because when the pastor has an offering call the first thing that comes out is a dollar bill.

Both men and women gossip, but women have turned it into an art form. If you meet a man that gossips too much, you call him Flip Flappin' Jones. If it's a woman you call her Motor Mouth Molly.

Husband: Honey, I had a revelation dream about you last night.
Wife: What was it all about?
Husband: Well, in the dream you were in deep prayer. You were asking the Lord to send you someone in your life that was more spiritual and deeper spiritually than you. Just then I saw a monkey appear on your shoulders, and you looked up toward the heavens and said, "Real funny, Lord." And I heard the Lord laugh.

Husband: Baby, last Sunday when you took your shoes off in church to get comfortable, I could have sworn I saw the Holy Spirit standing in the hall with his hand over his nose and a sign that said Marantha (Come quickly, Lord Jesus).

Wife: Hey honey, what do you call that thing on top of a house?
Husband: A chimney.
Wife: No, baby, the other thing.
Husband: Roof.
Wife: Here boy, nice boy, sit boy.

When I saw you from across the room I thought you were ugly. Now that I see you up close I'm positive.

Husband: Hey baby, you must eat a lot of pork.
Wife: Why do you say that?
Husband: Because you sure are pig headed at times.
Wife: That must mean you eat a lot of beef then because you give out a lot of bull.

One of the easiest ways to be remembered at church: Run up to one of the saints and shake his or her hand. While shaking the hand ask him what part of town he is from? Then tell him you are from Mars, also tell him we people from Mars don't use toilet paper, we use our hands.

You know for sure you have bad breath when everyone around you is wearing a gas mask and you're not.

You know that you're in the wrong church when the pastor calls for a human sacrifice and everyone turns and looks at you.

Hey man, I know the perfect heavy weight fight of the century. What's that? Evander Holyfield and Rodney Dangerfield.

You know you're old when the only inspiration you have to get up in the morning is to go the park to feed the pigeons.

You know you're old when you take the whole family out to the museum and the kids see a caveman and call him Daddy, and you look and think it does look like you.

When your wife is having a baby, you know it's time to get out of the delivery room when she digs her nails into your arms, looks at you, and says, "Just wait. I'm gonna get you for this."

Most parents want to give their children the things in life that they didn't have at that age. Why don't they get their children jobs?

You know you need to go to the dentist when the hardest thing you can eat is Jello unrefrigerated.

Hey, you know the difference between a cow and a bull? Well, with a cow you can milk, but with a bull you'll wind up in the hospital.

Well, a family ended up in child abuse court and the proceedings were just about over. The judge couldn't decide who was going to get custody of the child. So he turned to the little boy and asked, "Which parent would you like to live with?" He looked at both parents and knew he had been beaten by both, so he turned to the judge and said, "The Chicago White Soxs." "Why, the White Sox?" the judge said. And, the boy said, with a smile on his face, "Because the White Soxs don't beat anybody."

Hey! I heard that Hollywood is looking for a look-a-like for E.T. Why don't you go and try out for the part, and the best thing is you won't need any makeup.

You're in the Garden of Eden. Eve turns to Adam and says, "Adam, I sure liked that rib you gave me, but it sure could have used some barbecue sauce."

If you're at work, or school, and there is someone you would like to keep away from you and he comes over to you, ask him if he likes outer space, then tell him, "Over there is your space. This right here is my space. Stay out of my space."

Husband: Hey babe, do you want to know why Robin Hood's men were called merry men.
Wife: Why, sweetheart?
Husband: Because they had wives. Revelation, revelation, REVELATION!

Just remember Proverbs Chapter 15 Verse 13. A merry heart maketh a cheerful countenance but by sorrow of the heart the spirit is broken.